WITHDRAWN

101 Different Ways of Playing Solitaire

101
DIFFERENT WAYS
OF PLAYING SOLITAIRE
and Other Poems

*

Belle Randall

University of Pittsburgh Press

ISBN 0–8229–3261–x (cloth)
ISBN 0–8229–5235–1 (paper)

"A Wind Among the Singing Trees" first appeared in *Organ* and is used by permission.

"A Child's Garden of Gods," "Appropriate Postures," "San Quentin and Two Kinds of Conscience," "Genesis" (which appeared in slightly different form as "Afterward"), and "Attention Please" originally appeared in *Poetry*. Used by permission.

"The Confirmation of Our Inscrutable Friend," "Alice Reflections" (originally entitled "Alice Poems"), and "Gentlemen, the Bicycles Are Coming!" (originally entitled "The Bicycles Are Coming!") are reprinted with the permission of *The Southern Review*.

For my mother and the memory of my father

Many of these poems were written during the year I was a Wallace Stegner Fellow at Stanford University. I would like to thank the administrators of the Fellowship, and especially Donald Davie for his help in preparing the manuscript.

Contents

Part One

A Child's Garden of Gods

The summer that my mother fell
Into the hole that was herself,
We children sat like china dolls
Waiting mutely on a shelf
    For the horror to be done.

My father, who'd begun to drink
Jasmine from a turquoise cup,
Was practicing his yoga when
That dark mood swallowed Mama up.
    His trance was not undone.

When autumn came, like birds on wire,
Tilting forward in our rows,
We waited for our father to
Rise from his Oriental pose
    And save the fallen lady.

We stood around the stone-cold stove
The day her secrets gave her back.
She ran, and though her hair was damp,
And though her fingernails were black,
    Our mother still looked pretty.

She made a fire to thaw us out,
And after we were nicely browned,
She hugged us each, and told us all
About her travels underground.
    Her eyes were black as coffee.

She showed us bits of root and seed,
And other treasures found below:
Eyetooth of mole, old human bone,
And jewels she'd hidden long ago.
    Things buried always grow.

It's winter still. Our father sits
Cross-legged with an empty bowl.
Unmoved in the deserted yard,
He stares with perfect self-control
Into a wall of snow.

Appropriate Postures

Great Uncle's dead, that fool who'd play
The beaming mute or, worse, repeat
Himself for hours; who constantly
Forgot to put the toilet seat
Back down, in spite of our requests;
Whose special skill was spilling things;
Who lately, talking to himself,
Let out peculiar whimperings
And dark brown smells besides that wheeze
He'd always had. We sent him to
His room when we had company,
But out he'd creep, his thin old knees
Bent in self-apology.

Great Uncle's dead, that same old man
Who let his nose run when he wept
Last fall at our aunt's funeral,
While we all stood around and kept
On wishing him invisible.
Today we almost have our wish.
But this time as my family stands,
Extras in that solemn show,
Only Uncle seems to know
Exactly where to put his hands.

Tobias Rainwater, a Character from an Unfinished Novel, Dedicates His Book

I read once where that famous composer Bach dedicated all his great musical masterpieces to God. The words *fur Gott*, meaning "for God" in German, are supposedly written over and over by hand under every line he ever wrote.

If I had my way them same words would be written in English under every line of this book. That way, though others could read it if they liked, they'd know it was of no account to me if they did, or what they might think of it.

You don't have to be a genius to figure out that God is going to be less finicky than the general public. All you got to do is take a look around you at the world He invented and the number of people that haven't got the appetite for it.

America Has Seen Such Gods

America has seen such gods
Riding bareback to the stars
Above the plains on summer nights,
While in the back seats of our cars,
Beneath their coats, the children drowse,
Who've asked to be awakened when
We pass an outdoor movie screen,
Because they like to lift their faces to
Big faces in the sky.

Turning slowly in their seats,
They watch the underwater lights
Recede into the dark until
How far behind us now, America,
Those dreamlike horses plunge;
How smoothly and without a sound
Their riders, lifting up their arms,
Topple one by one

Above the dreaming continent
Whose children long ago agreed:
No one dies but Indians
And Indians are make-believe.

A Wind Among the Singing Trees

My father was a Cherokee,
Among his people called Shoo-shon,
A warrior name which means: You Fool,
Any Name You Call Me By Is Wrong.

My mother, Laughing In Their Faces, was
So beautiful she never needed mirrors,
But even in her fever had a beauty
Such as white men hope to put in words

And sometimes find in music. Look,
She cried, these beds with stainless rungs
Gleam and jangle like old bones. Tonight
When Rubber Gloves removed one of my lungs

I told him I would like more space to die in.
Instead he brings more magazines—
But death and I, though very old,
Will thrive among newfangled things.

Next morning Laughing In Their Faces died.
Among five fingers there is one
Which stands apart and is alone. To us,
A grieving man is like a thumb;

My father turned and walked through everyone.
Oh father, when I walk down corridors
Of public buildings late at night, or peek
Inside the new museum's doors

To where, in rooms as white as wards,
Statues file in endless rows
Like amputees from long forgotten wars,
Sometimes I glimpse the way it snows

Across the prairies of The Holding Breath
Where every man is named Shoo-shon
And laughing in their faces sings
Any name you call me by is wrong.

Gentlemen, the Bicycles Are Coming!

Gentlemen, the bicycles are coming!
In silver, slanting rows like rain
They ride the moonlit highways toward
The towns where we lie dreaming.

Beyond the icy windowpane
As if a tuning fork were striking stars
We hear a spray of tiny bells,
Cold, metallic, ringing,

And pushing back the curtains see
Stainless-steel handlebars
Like skeletons of scavengers
Upon us in the darkness winging.

There is a shaft of freezing air;
A moment when their headlights shine
Into our eyes; the bedroom walls
Are white, electrified, and gleaming.

The bicycles come sweeping down
The asphalt slope in starlit columns,
Pass the house and dwindle to
A flash of faint italics leaning

Round a distant curve, and Gentlemen—
They're gone! The curtains close,
And darkness spills across the shelves
Whose books, like tombs, contain their meaning.

Suppose

the universe is all a setup
and everybody knows but you
and this is your first clue.

The Confirmation of Our Inscrutable Friend

Into the chambers of the Buddha's ear
He speaks, who when the phone rings does not answer.
All morning long his door is locked, whose gaze
    Is fixed on Buddha Nature.

The open *I Ching* by his sunlit plate
At tea portends arrivals imminent.
Though friends, inviting us to wait, did not
    Divine which way he went,

A stick of musk still glowing in its jar
At dusk suggests he's stepped outside and strolls
The twilight boulevards below, behind
    Dark glasses and a rose.

Escorted past his rooms as darkness falls,
We glimpse his monogram on velvet towels,
And pausing in the moonlit drive observe
    His silent, waiting Rolls.

And so it goes—the ticket for a train
That leaves, distinguished by a vacant seat;
The wife, producing signatures, who hasn't
    Seen him for a week;

The dragon-headed walking stick; the ornate
Letterhead; the gold initialed ring;
The rooms in which we find his character
    Engraved on everything;

The thousand certain clues which lead us to
A garden where an ancient Bo tree grows,
And leave us feeling for the body in
    A heap of empty clothes.

Alice Reflections

I   The Looking Glass

Black kittens with their sweet dark faces
And tiny claws recall the roses
In a dream. All afternoon I've thought
Of water and the way it closes

Over things, have looked within
The looking glass whose polished face reveals
A glimpse into a somber world
The face of things conceals.

Two parlors at its surface meet
And stand like bookends back to back.
In everything—a game of chess,
A pack of cards, this world and that—

I think of things symmetrical—
Sinister, nonsensical—
The Red Queen and the Black—
Opposite, and yet identical.

But though beyond the glass I've seen
All things the other way around,
And in a deeper sleep have found
A wonderland underground,

The walls as I awaken close
Like sunlit water on my dream.
Oh tailor of the universe,
How well you've hid its seam!

II *The Riverbank*

It's as she learned who hid her secrets
Beneath the surface of the lake:
Things become transparent when in shadow
Which in sunlight are opaque.

Then Dreamer, shut your eyes and drift
Through shapes that bloom against the black
Into a realm whose vastness makes
The outside of your face its back.

Past roots as white as scar, descend
Into the belly of the earth
Where dead things mixed with rain secrete
Peculiar odors of rebirth.

No need to linger here, while through
Your tears a tiny garden gleams
Before you in the sunlight like
The pieces of a broken thing.

Suppose that there are roses growing
Beside the river where you sleep,
Their petals dark and red as those
Behind the door at which you weep.

And as the latch clicks open, ask:
On which side of this tiny door
Bloom the roses for which roses
    Bloom in metaphor?

Decision

For Rod Taylor

I look into my best friend's face
and say good-bye. I clean out
my bank account, requesting all
that it contains ($300.65)
in crisp one hundred dollar bills
and change. This I place
in a shoe box kept beneath my bed,
strip the bedding off,
and picking up a butcher knife,
rip the mattress like a carcass, seam to seam,
pull the stuffing out, and break the legs for kindling.

I rummage through my drawers and find
my Greta Garbo hat, marriage license,
and certificate of birth.
Heaping these with the mattress and the box
in a stolen Safeway cart,
I roll it all outside.

It's dusk. In the yard behind the house
my mother, who is waiting,
has already struck the match.
We watch the fire catch.
Then slowly we undress,
discarding first our coats and hats,
then shoes and socks, leaving on
only the thin cotton dresses
we will need to warm us through the night.

For a moment as we kerosene
the Safeway cart, it turns into
an ancient baby carriage, ablaze
against the dark. We watch until
a distant siren warns us that
some neighbor must have called
the firemen or cops,

then turn and walk together up the block,
thinking of how much it's worth
not to know
what's going to happen next.

Familiarity

After reading Denise Levertov

How well we know this woman—know
not her secrets, secrets are
always a bit theatrical
and have to do with public roles—
but something much more intimate
and dark—familiar as five moles
peppering the upper arm
on which you leaned in childhood's warm
pajamas, gazing at
bright pictures turning in the lap
of someone whom you did not love
because you were too close for that;
the casually revealed shock
of hair beneath the arms of women
heavy with maturity, who lean
on shopping carts at dusk, and talk
of this one's hysterectomy
and that one's uterus,
oblivious
to blushes rising in the cheeks
of children they offend
by having made their peace
with rumbling pipes of birth and bowel;
a lewd dependency that droops
beneath the belly of the sow
where white hairs, soft as down, disclose
a vulgar map of pink and brown;
a closeness like the closed tile room
where once, behind a cloud of steam,
my mother, rising from her bath,
reached out to comfort me—but I—
in that sudden grasp perceiving

old, most intimate connections with
her private chambers—twisted free, and fled
into the night air's cold

slap of freedom, gulping breath.

Clairvoyant

A dyed redhead with one glass eye
and alcoholic breath
is lurching through the cocktail crowd
proclaiming loudly, "I am myth!"

We recognize at once
our local poetess,
who hides in everything she writes
like a blood spot in a handkerchief

the peekaboo of death. "Ahah!"
The artificial eye
revolving like a searchlight swings,
I swear it does, around the room.

Too large for life, too bold, too blue,
unfeeling though it gleams
possibilities of pain
our seeing eyes cannot

imagine or contain,
it roams, it roams. Meanwhile
the other eye (small and inflamed)
is fixed on me;

the pugilistic face,
battered with experience,
is thrust in mine; the voice,
hoarse with having strained

for emphasis, inquiring
(our conversation having turned
from myth to supernatural things)
and what of me?

Do I believe in ghosts
who come back from the grave
to rattle
relatives and topple hats?

"No," I say,
"my dreams of immortality
are much more grand than that."

"Exactly so!"
Her teeth clench as she laughs.
Apparently I've found a friend in this
incurable insomniac

who often in the night
weary of the world
she paces half
in blindness, half in sight,

has yearned for death,
believing that upraised at last
both her eyes
        shall shine like glass.

To Antony, from Cleopatra

Sweetest where her seed is kept
And wrapped the way a mother's arms
Are wrapped about a newborn babe,
The evening is a dark red rose
Whose petals layer on layer close
Around the hush, their lushness kept
   In heart within heart within heart.

Husky, bluesy, brimming, dark—
The city sings, and in her throat
The harbor swells, a vast Amen,
The sunset gleams, a gospel note,
The night is soul turned inside out,
A paradise whose lights recede,
   Arc beyond arc beyond arc.

On Hallelujah Boulevard,
Discarding silken scarves at dusk,
The city struts, a gorgeous slut
Who slithers and who shakes until
Her thighs glitter like black gutters
And her eyes are alleyways
   Where thieves whisper *Quick!* in the dark.

Singing:
   I'm the *Honey could'ja, could'ja*
In the Hootchy-Kootchy-Kootcher;
I'm a temptress, I'm a tigress, I'm a tart;
   I'm a woman with thick hips
   And thickly painted lips.
Oh Honey, smear your fingertips
In the ache of my innermost part.

The secrets there laid bare at last
As thighs like moonlit bridges part,
Infants curl and sailors moor
In the milk white arms of girls
Who rock them while the city sleeps,
An ancient sow with drooping teats
   And love folded into her dark.

Till like a night made vivid by
The tears that shine in Egypt's eyes,
Everything that's old and cheap
Is transformed by something deep—
A rose, unfolded from the heart
Of innocence its scarlet layers
   Of art without art without art.

Attention Please

The secret of all life is this:
One day you will become a kite,
Your flesh grown tissue-paper thin,
Your face, a wad of crumpled bed sheet, white;

And on that day—your rib cage arched,
Your arms and legs spread out and bending back
Until they form a cross of bone—
Twirling slowly, you'll ascend.

Perhaps some toy blue morning, carried like
A scrap of paper in the wind
Round the world, while all the scenes below
Pass through your suddenly transparent skin.

Perhaps at night, while in your darkened room,
Your wife and children at the window
Calling out, "But Daddy—," see
You sailing like a ship across the moon.

What does it matter when? The point is,
In the face of this all personal desires,
All topical despairs—the children's teeth,
The dissertation, the divorce—

Matter less than this: the way,
Turning in the door last night at dusk,
As if someone had called your name,
You felt the tugging of a distant string;

Or why so many poems contain
Images of flimsy things—an old
Meat wrapper scraping down the sidewalk
In the dark; white curtains lifting in the wind.

Part Two

101
Different Ways
of Playing Solitaire

Solitaire:
A gem in a setting; a large stud;
a game for one person; a recluse;
an extinct bird allied to the
Dodo.
    Walker's Rhyming Dictionary

I   Introduction

Mrs. Woo slumps at her mirror.
"Look at me," she says, "I'd nothing else to do
so like a dope
I went and cut my hair."

It's six P.M.
Pork chops fry; incense burns.
We eat in silence,
after which, taking turns,
we do the dishes.

"It's not the hair one minds so much," she says.
"The hair will grow.
It's—ohhh,
nothing ever happens here."

Sometimes she thinks we ought to move, she says.
It's either that or move him out
(She rolls her eyes toward the ceiling)—
Lately she can't sleep
without the radio and lights
what with him up there all night long
playing solitaire.
The sound is what she minds the most
(She grasps my sleeve as I am leaving)
That awful shuffling, she says,
why, in the dark
it sounds like someone breathing.

2

The number's gone; the name is worn.
The other tenants only know
The man who plays at solitaire
By an initial, Mr. O.—

But Mrs. Woo has passed his open door,
And peeked inside his dingy room,
Distinguishing amid the scents
Of mildewed magazines and cheap perfume

A tacky wartime calendar
("An odd detail—What can it *mean?*")—
Betty Grable in a bathing suit
And patent pumps salutes America,

And though she's never seen his face,
She's seen him there: his back to her,
His shoulders hunched, his cigarette
A red glow on the table where

Afterwards she hears his hands
Laying out long corridors
Of cards, as she continues down
The endless line, the numbered doors.

3

It's not as if we never played at cards—
Canasta, rummy, 21—
Ours is a standard deck:
808
Bicycle
Rider Back
"Well, look at this," says Mrs. Woo,
Showing me the back of one:

Approaching from a universe
More old and intricate than lace
An angel on a bicycle
Lends skill and chance the mark of grace.

She holds it in the light a while,
Lost deep inside that dark design
Whereby things secular become
Conveyances of things divine.

4

I dream: a woman standing at her mirror
Is saying, "Sometimes when I talk to you
I get the feeling it is I
    Am playing solitaire."

Behind her in the darkened room, a man
Answers as he lays the cards face down,
"How come you never look at things
    The other way around?"

5

The evening darkens. In the lobby of
The Brown Hotel in Chinatown
Cigars are lit. A television glows.
Beside a dusty palm, old men

With freckle-spattered fingers doze.
Sifting through our talk, the sound
Of laughter and of gangster shows
Is comforting as falling rain.

Listening, one thinks of how
As faces turn toward lighted screens
In darkened rooms on upper floors,
The populations of our dreams

Divide and multiply like cells
Into a myriad of tiny selves
Whose blue light spills, whose music swells
Down hallways in a hundred brown hotels.

II Genesis

1

My evenings are recurring dreams
Of winding stairs and narrow halls
At dusk. I journey toward
A distant door where strings of glass,

Twirling in the gloom,
Send sprays of colored light
Drifting like the universe across
The secrets of a single room.

I push the beaded curtains back
And Genesis occurs:
The Mysteries of Creation sift
And tumble past me in a blurred

Profusion on the papered walls,
Dwindle and resolve themselves
In scattered, gleaming stars.
My eyes adjust; I am aware

Of that sole star, myself,
An empty room, an oval mirror, one
More night, one hundred one
Ways of playing solitaire.

2

On the second landing as I climbed
One night I happened to look down:
Encoiled by the gleaming banister,
Revolving in the blue light far below,
The threadbare carpet in the lobby of
The Brown Hotel in Chinatown
With every step became
More roselike and more sinister—
A rose, which as I kept on
Climbing upward, looking down,
Appeared to close—though I suppose
It would have seemed to open if
Approached the other way around.

3

The Chinese children on the stairs
And those who live behind these doors

Are mostly numbers, just like cards,
But here and there a face appears:

The ivory chess piece, Madam Wang
(By accident stuck in our game),

Who every evening dusts a shelf
Of photos of her former self,

Explaining on the public phone,
"A local address, not my home . . ."

The desk clerk, Fong—half blind, half deaf,
As buck-toothed as the letter "F,"

Who saves for every resident
His share of mail to "Occupant";

And, of course, our authoress,
Blond, divorcée, twenty-six,

Misrepresented by these facts—
North Beach girl in army slacks—

Her neighbors do not know her name;
In secrecy she dreams of fame.

4

Slanting through the window shades
Late sunlight turns my cluttered room
Into an antique, amber photograph.
Jars of face cream, bottles of perfume,
Gleaming on the chest of drawers,
Begin to cool as evening blues
The mirrored world at which I stare,
Listening to the surf of passing cars,
Watching as between two posts
The tilted oval glass
Signals in the darkness to the stars:

5

Water roars. Behind the wall
The next-door tenant, Mrs. Woo,
With whom I share the rumbling bowl
Of ancient toilet, chain and ball,
And "privileges" of kitchenette,
Fills the claw-foot tub we rent.

There's no way out—when Christ said Love
Thy Neighbor, this is who he meant.

6

Mabel Woo,
age 49,
onetime chorus girl
(Johnny Lotus Yum-Yum Girl Review,
Chinese Capers, 1942),
stage name: Roxie Starr,
now Rexall Drugs cashier,

at age 18, elected Queen
of Chinese New Year 1938
(a yellowed clipping shows her wearing
ermine and a bathing suit,
waving from a dragon float),
set out for Hollywood to be a star—

hard, always, for an Oriental girl,
impossible during The War
("Too young for Shangri-la,
too old for *South Pacific*—
everybody took me for a Jap");
she wound up in a storefront school
teaching ballroom dance and tap;

her only speaking part—
a 1940s Charlie Chan
("A flop, but even so,"
seeing it in *TV Guide* last week,
"it lasted longer than my marriage did").
About the latter and the man—
"Ah so!" she quips, and will not speak.

And now APPEARING NIGHTLY in
A Faded Robe
across whose purple plains
red cowboys swing gold lariats,
transistor under arm,
sleep mask perched on head,
Mabel Woo, age 49,
is on her way to bed.

She hovers in my doorway while I work,
pockets drooping like an old sow's teats
with matchbooks, Q-Tips and a few
tobacco-clung imported sweets,
not to mention Sleep-Eze
and more potent drugs
to aid her in the dark
oncoming passage into sleep.

7

How many midnights—"Bedtime snack?"—
She's pushed my door ajar a crack,
Inquiring if I want to share
The meager portion labeled hers
Inside our hive-top Frigidaire.

As late sometimes as one A.M.
(A book beneath her arm, an ashtray
Like an alms plate in her hand—
"I saw your light, may I come in?"),
She settles on my davenport,
Her cigarette a firefly spark,
The book unopened in her lap,
Her restless hands as thin as smoke
Rising from the red-hot ash
With which she pokes a crooked path
Through burnt-out matchsticks in a glass.

But though I guess the fear concealed
Inside these empty gestures like
A stain inside a glove,
I confess I'm filled with terror
When, stirring ashes, she begins,
"Aside from you,
                    there's nobody I love . . ."

8

Who is this Oriental pearl,
Mixed syllable of woe and rue,
Who haunts the dark side of my room?

Between the stars and me, what moon
Rising casts a pall of blue
Across these pages as I write?

Through lids so taut they seem to hurt,
Gazing, stoic, through the snow
That falls across the Late Late Show,

She mirrors my fullness in the gloom,
Cupped in dark, her oval face,
Small and empty as a spoon.

LET'S TAKE A STROLL DOWN MEMORY LANE . . .

She magnifies

a paid announcement that recalls
The Hits Of 1944,
Benny Goodman, Harry James,
Mood Indigo
of world war,
a *Sentimental Journey* toward
nights on leave in brown hotels
in rooms with names like Roseland, Island
Paradise, and Shangri-la,
where couples did not move at all,
but stood together in a drift
of light, and balls made of a million
mirrors revolved, and songs—

and songs like *Stardust* played all night.

10

Her youth seems larger than my own,
Its musicals and mysteries
Dramas glimpsed behind a door
Through which I am too young to go:

I cannot see beyond The War.
In memory, that final door
Opens on a bedroom where,
Framed by darkness, bathed in light,
My mother is a movie star.

Each evening as our story ends
She rises from my outstretched hands,
Blows a kiss, and turning takes
Away the light that she lets in.

Behind her in a grown-up world
Big people stay up late, whose talk
Still whispers in the dark of things
Larger than I've ever felt:
Temptation! Conflict! Intrigue! Guilt!

Gleaming on the chest of drawers
Beside my bed, and autographed—
"A G.I. sends Love & Kisses to
His two best girls"—my father's face

Is lit by passing cars, his eyes
Projected on the wider screen
Beyond my window where a searchlight,
Climbing God's dark kingdom, seeks
His face at large among the stars.

Childhood and Hollywood—
      twin myths
That shrink into a star of light
And dwindle on the TV screen;
An aging Chink with has-been chic
Who waits for me to say good-night.

III   A Game for One Person

1

"What did you say?" I say
tonight. It's early yet.
I'm standing at the window
with a flashlight and a pocket mirror
contriving to become the evening star
for someone singular
who lives across the bay.

"I said that nothing happens here."

Upstairs the man who knows one hundred one
different ways of playing solitaire
shuffles all the cards and lays them out again.

Here, I raise my star
by standing on a kitchen chair.

2

Mine is a better room than some.
I have a view. Those thousand lights
across the bay are Berkeley, where
my friend the old professor lives
who at this very moment might
be pausing in his work to share
some highly personal merriment
with no one but the evening star.

3

The old professor's working on a book.
If it is any good
how inappropriate his picture
on the flyleaf's going to look.

Not that it matters much
if it doesn't, if it does:

Look into mirrors, look out at stars;
address your thoughts to anyone
who's gone for long enough, and soon
how like yourself, and yet
how starlike they become.

4

"Seeing me, Confucius say,
Truth Seeker take for granted
Very thing he cannot see
About himself—"

                "What's that?" I ask.

She answers, "Chump,
Your eyes are slanted."

5

As Betty Grable flings herself across
As Betty Grable in one of her famous snits
As on one hundred television sets
Betty Grable weeps
("He promised me I had the part
and like a dope . . .")

As on one hundred television sets
Betty Grable sinks
into one flounced white chair
("They told me he liked dames with class
so like a dope
I went and dyed my hair . . .")

As Betty Grable,
flouncing through a doorway, flings
her sling-back pump against a three-way mirror
("What does he take me for—a dope?
Come on, Sis, let's grab
the next train out of here . . .")

As in the Brown Hotel in Chinatown
from every room a voice intones,
"You're so cute when you get mad"

I read my old professor's book
and drink a glass of milk alone.

6

Sound of slippers clapping up a hall.
"Good-night again, I'm on my way to bed.

GOOD-NIGHT MISS LITERARY-TYPE, I SAID."

Sound of slippers clapping down a hall.
                    Ker-plunk, ker-plunk,
the slippers fall beside a bed.
A bedspring, squeaking loudly, gives.
A pause, and then:

"Good-night, good-night, ah nuts—
I might as well
be shouting through
                    a megaphone into
          the ear
   of someone dead."

7

EXTRA! EXTRA!
Last night the secrets of the universe
were cracked
by an old professor and a girl
who, spilling money as they ran,
vanished in a black sedan—

a quiet pair, friends say,
who lived as you and I
until one day,
leaving life behind them, they
absconded with its meaning—

clever thieves
who leave behind the jewels
and steal their wicked gleaming!

8

Across the bay, the old professor
rises from that desk in which
unknown to colleague, wife or child he keeps
a stash of Hi-Ho Crackers and
unfinished manuscript, and as
at one A.M.
the streets likewise
belong to him,
decides to walk in them,

and as he walks he speaks
and every word is meant
straight from the bottom of his heart
to Nietzsche, Kierkegaard, or Kant,

when with a sudden swoosh
of radio and lights
a big convertible sweeps past
full of modern couples who
observe him there in retrospect—

an old man talking to himself,
a bald man looking for his hat.

I saw this in a dream.
I was so furious I wept.
I went to Mrs. Woo.
"About that hat," I said,

"I do not think you comprehend
the importance of the work
we're doing here.
Do you realize we have
amassed a hundred different ways
of playing solitaire?"
I had a suitcase
and one hundred
packs of cards.
I showed her every one.
Mrs. Woo was standing at the mirror.
When I was done
she did not move her eyes at all
but very slowly turned her head.
I saw she had a gun.
"Thank you very much," she said,
firing, "And now you know
one hundred one."

9

I waken as the shot rings out.
It's two A.M.
The bar downstairs has closed.
Far down the moonlit street
a jazz musician goes,
like Orpheus,
into the underworld.

Then come,
there's no one here but me,
talking to my mirror, and
behind a beaded curtain—Mr. Big,
absorbed in solitaire.

10

Let us be alone
and in so being be
with him who never was
alone but he was with
Nietzsche, Kierkegaard, or Kant—
One need but think of any one
of a hundred bald old men,
to walk down moonlit streets and chant
their names until—at last!
Ah, my shining English teachers,
Oh, my middle-aged professors—
Look into mirrors, look out at stars—
sometimes no matter where I look
behind me in the dark I hear your hands
turning through the pages of a book,
while I, no less alone tonight,
think of you and how
although there really are
one hundred different ways
of playing solitaire,
surely this—the way we share—
is the most singular; and this
seems at once so sad, so odd
and wonderful I now address
a message I shall never send

from the bottom of my heart
and straight to you
my solitary man: Tonight!
Wear dark glasses and a smoke red rose
and in the car you use to do your crimes in
black and soundless as
a river in the moonlight glide
through back alleys and deserted
tunnels to the parking lot outside
The Palace of Fine Art

        where in my Edith Sitwell cloak
        in my Greta Garbo guise
        in my Isadora Duncan garb
        in this garbled world
        of INDIVIDUALITY,
                  I hide.

And we will climb the winding stair,
and we will walk the narrow hall,
and step into that darkness where,
although we may not see his face,
we may stand behind the chair
of the man who knows

                101

different ways of playing solitaire.
And in that holy hush till dawn,

Arranged in perfect trinity,
you, the elder; I, the younger;
   He,
the master of all solitaire,
shall speak no word, but breathe the air
until the very air we breathe,
we breathe in unity,
watching as his restless fingers,
yellow with tobacco stain,
laden down with dust-encrusted
rings of opal, sapphire, jade—
shuffle, shuffle, shuffle through
infinities of loneliness,
and from the chaos of the cards
unfold an endless universe
where all things are at last revealed
and even red and black
shown to be harmonious,
as our souls
fly out across the city in the dawn—

purified, anonymous.

11

And yet I would not go. I am afraid.
What if, while we are standing there,
his body should begin to sag
slowly as a bag of sand
sideways in the chair,
lurch and slide
crashing through the furniture,
and as I reach to catch his sleeve
the cloth rips and his body rolls
open like an empty hand
before me in the moonlight where
his jaw falls open with a clatter
of false teeth, fool's gold, or wire;
revolving upward in his head
like numbers in a slot machine
his eyeballs spin
from zero to oblivion, and stare
vacantly and outward always
back at me—what if
the man who plays at solitaire is dead?
What then?

Then I will turn to you,
and if you turn to leave,
then I will turn to Mrs. Woo,
and drag her down,
and clutch her by the sleeve,
and plead:

> Pay those people banging at the door
> anything, but bury him,
> bury him, and promise me
> we'll never be alone again.

IV Fusion

1

Riddled

like a   body with a   submachine gun
BLAST the night   is full of   radios and
exclamation   marks and   words like
          FLASH
bulbs and champagne corks   POPPING   pills and
prices SLASHED and   DROPPING   bombs and
SMACK and windows   CRASHING Jesus   SAVES and
SPEED   freaks FLASHING sirens   and revolving
lights on   SHINING RED and   Black & White
cars careening   toward the   spot
where I remember   I've been   SHOT
(the bullet lodged precisely where
Luther said that God lives squarely
         underneath the left
         nipple)
and I touch it and   my fingertips are
         black and wet
and hit concrete amid a crush
of jackpots paying off in CASH
and CRACKpots wearing paper hats
waving Happy Doomsday plaques
as someone says get back get back
and tears a swatch out of my dress
and uses it to try to catch
the universe
         that's leaking out
         the black
         hole
that punctuates my flesh.

2

Words like "Acapulco Gold"
and "softly parted lips"
are slurred into APOCALYPSE
and here at "CBS Reports"
all history
    beyond control
       is spilling backward
         like a roll
           of toilet paper
          down
             The White House Steps
as someone on
    the HOT LINE quips
"Y'know, this could be serious."

3
Mrs. Woo, is that you?

4

Rising like a coffin lid,
I sit upright in bed.
Mrs. Woo is at the mirror.
She very slowly turns her head.
And suddenly I understand:
She's come for me because I'm dead.

She holds a hand mirror to my lips.
My breathing does not steam the glass.
My cheeks are white and streaked with ash.
"But can it really be?" I ask.
"Pinch yourself and see," she says;
My fingers melt right through the flesh.

"No time for explanations now—
The meter's running on the cab."
I float behind her as I'm bid
Across the rooftop to the fire
Escape into a waiting—"Black,"
I notice as we leave the curb,
"Is not the color of a cab."

"Courthouse steps, and make it fast."
She sits in front, eyes fixed ahead.
And suddenly I understand:
The Judgment Day is come at last,
And I'm among the risen dead.
"But what will it be like?" I ask.

"Death? (a cool, ironic laugh)
It's much the same as life—except,
Of course, one needn't be afraid
Of death. Death's as common here
As walking through a door at dusk
Or winding an electric clock.

"You've died before; you'll die again,
And every death in retrospect
will seem as insignificant
(Giving me a backward glance)
As that author whom you haven't read,
That neighbor whom you've never met.

"You'll learn that death's as natural here
(She stops to light a cigarette),
As air; one in- and exhales death.
The only thing you need to be
Afraid of here—
                    But what's the matter,
                    Dear? You look as startled as
                    A baby drawing its first breath."

5

City Hall, five A.M.
granite steps, thumb-smudged doors,
grimy in the grim gray light
as Crime Lab photographs
enlarged in grainy black and white.

6

Zap!
Fingers raise a crooked shade
and clenching bring a fist
down with force
             upon a desk
strewn with paper
             clips and cups
spewing ash and crumpled butts
on pages ringed with coffee stains
as someone rising
             blurred behind
the thick glass window where I strain
to hear what he is saying shouts
I tell ya Sam
             we've nailed our man
the arrest's as good as made
this time we're gonna make it stick
he's one foot in the grave

while another man
             whose name
it strikes me just before the light
illuminates the inside of my skull
and everything goes black
             is Spade
wisecracks as he kneels above
my body in the doorway: Bang
             Little Girl you're dead
the minute that you think
             you got it made.

7

Clubbed or blackjacked,
clubbed or blackjacked,
somebody explains.
I hold my head.
My temples throb with pain.

A flashlight darts across the darkness past
an office door, a pinup calendar,
a cluttered table where
it hesitates
encircling in light the words:

101
Official Rules
For Inmates Locked in Solitaire

Zap!
Showing me a metal star,
pulling out a wooden chair . . .

A naked light bulb
dangles like a hanging man
above a cluttered table where
a man behind a black cigar
shoves before me photographs
saying, "Was it him?" and "Was it him?"

Squinting in the glare
I try to bring in focus
faces I have never met,
acquaintances and friends
facing front and profile left,
their features sullen, hardened, set,
soiled as the fingertips
dipped in ink and pressed
in print beside each photograph.

"Take a gander at these two—"
Slapping down the old professor's
photograph and one I hardly
recognize as Mrs. Woo,
circa 1942—
"Was it him? Was it him?
Think again," he says. I do.

Words like "booked" and "booking"
mingle in my brain.
A clown, led handcuffed from the room,
looks back at me in sympathy,
a painted teardrop, greasepaint blue,
sliding down his cheek like rain.

"But I don't understand," I say at length.
"It must be almost dawn, and it
was none of them, none of them,
for no one's done me any wrong."

The minute that I've said the words,
afraid that they're too strong,
I rise about to—
                    Zap!
                    Somebody pulls a switch
                    and suddenly

                                the lights come on.

The old professor at the window turns.
His eyes are moist and fond.
"Okay Little Girl," he says,
"Your Judgment Day is done.

Still don't understand, Sweetheart—?"

He lifts the window shade
and very, very gradually
an *awful* light begins to dawn.

8

I must have been adrift some place
A million miles away in space,
Have searched its mirror a million times,
And never even seen that face;

Have climbed the narrow labyrinth
In icy spirals through the night
A million landings, turns, and flights,
And never even seen the light;

Have heard my steps resounding down
The dusty hall a million years,
And never even realized
That awesome roaring in my ears

Is not the sound of silence, it's
A flurried rustling in the wings
Of angels, gathered in a hush,
To witness this, behind the scenes;

Have dreamed about The Great White Way,
Stars and roses, fame and dust,
A million childish dreams, and never
Guessed: the old professor thrusts

A bunch of roses in my arms;
Mrs. Woo adjusts the mike.
The curtain rises and I'm thrust
Into my glory and my light.

9

Worth least of all or more than kings
Though numberless I have no face.
At my gate all journeys end.
Birth and death in me take place.

Rank and file encounter me
To form a circle's perfect grace.
One palm contains a rose, and one
A nail driven through the flesh.

To guess the riddle that I am
Write the name in this blank space:

_____

Of him you hold most dear, and look—
The card you're holding is the Ace.

10

And Genesis occurs . . .
The Mysteries of Creation sift
And tumble past me in a blurred

Profusion on the papered walls,
Dwindle and resolve themselves
In scattered, gleaming stars.
My eyes adjust; I am aware

Of that sole star—the sun,
An empty room, an oval mirror,
The dawning of one hundred one
New ways of playing solitaire.

PITT POETRY SERIES

COLOPHON

This book is set in the Linotype cutting of Baskerville types.
It was printed from the type by Heritage Printers, Inc., on
Warren's Olde Style antique wove paper on a Miehle 41 flat-
bed letterpress. The character of the type is in large part de-
pendent upon the pressing of the type into the soft paper,
and the evenness with which it is done is a measure of the
pressman's skill. This book was designed by Gary Gore; the
pressman was Howard L. Lewis.